Luisa Rose
Lustige Tanzspiele
Ausmalbuch für Erwachsene

Bibliografische Information der Deutschen Nationalbibliothek:
Die Deutsche Nationalbibliothek verzeichnet diese Publikation in der
Deutschen Nationalbibliografie; detaillierte bibliografische
Daten sind im Internet über http://dnb.dnb.de abrufbar.

© 2016 Luisa Rose; 1. Auflage
Covergrafik, Texte & Illustrationen © 2016 Luisa Rose

Herstellung und Verlag: BoD – Books on Demand, Norderstedt

ISBN: 9783743104273

Inhalte

When I was a Young Girl	Seite	4
Jenny Jones		11
Green Gravel		15
Milking Pails		18
Here Comes Three Dukes a-Riding		27
Old Roger		30
We are the Rovers		32
Poor Mary Sits a-Weeping		36

WHEN I WAS A YOUNG GIRL

When I was a schoolgirl, a schoolgirl, a schoolgirl.
When I was a schoolgirl, oh this way went I.

WHEN I WAS A YOUNG GIRL

And this way and that way and this way and that way
When I was a schoolgirl, oh this way went I.

WHEN I WAS A YOUNG GIRL Contd

When I was a teacher, a teacher, a teacher,
When I was a teacher, oh this way went I.
And this way & that way & this way & that way
When I was a teacher, oh this way went I.

When I had a sweetheart, a sweetheart, a sweetheart
When I had a sweetheart, oh this way went I.
And this way & that way & this way & that way
When I had a sweetheart, oh this way went I.

When I had a husband, a husband, a husband
When I had a husband, oh this way went I.
And this way & that way & this way & that way
When I had a husband, oh this way went I

When I was a young girl Continued

When I took in washing, oh washing, oh washing,
When I took in washing, oh this way went I.
And this way & that way & this way & that way
When I took in washing, oh this way went I.

When my baby died, oh died, oh died,
When my baby died, how sorry was I.
And this way & that way & this way & that way
When my baby died, oh this way went I.

When my husband died, oh died, oh died,
When my husband died, how sorry was I.
And this way & that way & this way & that way
When my husband died, oh this way went I.

 # JENNY JONES

POOR·JENNY·JONES

Mother
Oh! Jenny is washing, washing, washing,
Oh! Jenny is washing, you can't see her now.

Suitors
We've come to see poor Jenny Jones, Jenny Jones, Jenny Jones.
We've come to see poor Jenny Jones, how is she now?

Mother
Oh! Jenny is starching, starching, starching,
Oh! Jenny is starching, you can't see her now.

Suitors
We've come to see poor Jenny Jones, Jenny Jones, Jenny Jones,
We've come to see poor Jenny Jones how is she now?

Poor Jenny is dying

JENNY JONES CON^{TD}

MOTHER
Oh! Jenny is ironing, ironing, ironing,
Oh! Jenny is ironing, you can't see her now.

SUITORS
We've come to see poor Jenny Jones, Jenny Jones,
We've come to see poor Jenny Jones & how is she now?

MOTHER
Poor Jenny is ill, is ill, is ill,
Poor Jenny is ill, you can't see her now.

SUITORS
We've come to see poor Jenny Jones, Jenny Jones,
We've come to see poor Jenny Jones, & how is she now?

MOTHER
Poor Jenny is dying, is dying, is dying,
Poor Jenny is dying, you can't see her now.

SUITORS
We've come to see poor Jenny Jones, Jenny Jones,
We've come to see poor Jenny Jones & how is she now?

MOTHER
Poor Jenny is dead, dead, dead,
Poor Jenny is dead, you can't see her now.

ALL
There's red for the Soldiers & blue for the sailors,
And black for the mourners of poor Jenny Jones.

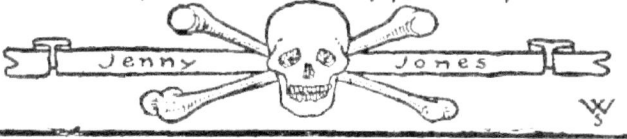

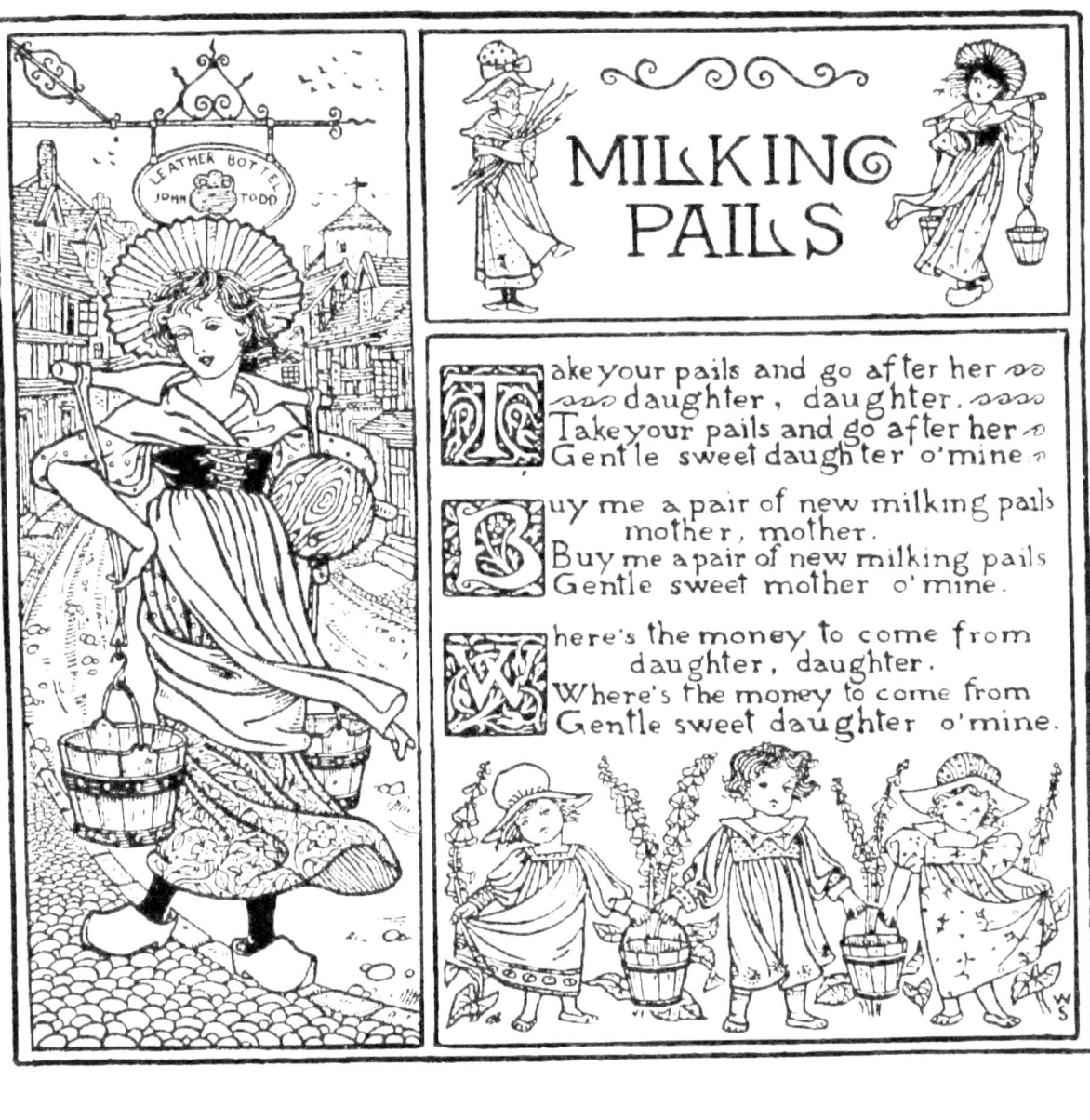

MILKING PAILS

Take your pails and go after her
 daughter, daughter.
Take your pails and go after her
Gentle sweet daughter o' mine.

Buy me a pair of new milking pails
 mother, mother.
Buy me a pair of new milking pails
Gentle sweet mother o' mine.

Where's the money to come from
 daughter, daughter.
Where's the money to come from
Gentle sweet daughter o' mine.

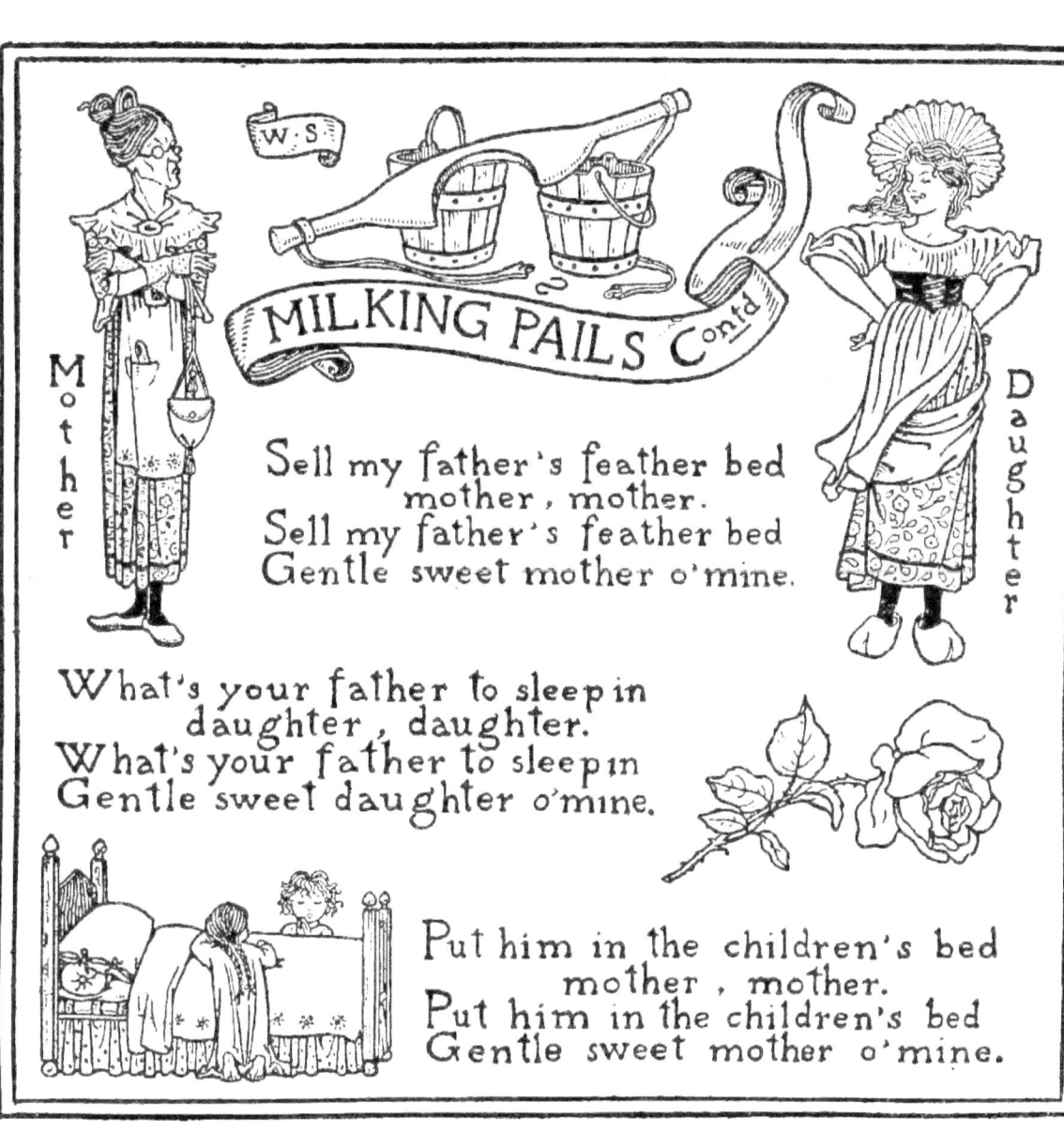

MILKING PAILS Cont'd

Mother — **Daughter**

Sell my father's feather bed
mother, mother.
Sell my father's feather bed
Gentle sweet mother o'mine.

What's your father to sleep in
daughter, daughter.
What's your father to sleep in
Gentle sweet daughter o'mine.

Put him in the children's bed
mother, mother.
Put him in the children's bed
Gentle sweet mother o'mine.

MILKING PAILS

Where shall the children go to [sleep]
   daughter, daughter.
Where shall the children go to [sleep]
Gentle sweet daughter o'mine.

Put them in the pig stye
   mother, mother.
Put them in the pig stye
Gentle sweet mother o'mine.

What shall the pigs lay in
   daughter, daughter.
What shall the pigs lay in
Gentle sweet daughter o'mine

Put them in the washing tub
   mother, mother
Put them in the washing tub
Gentle sweet mother o'mine.

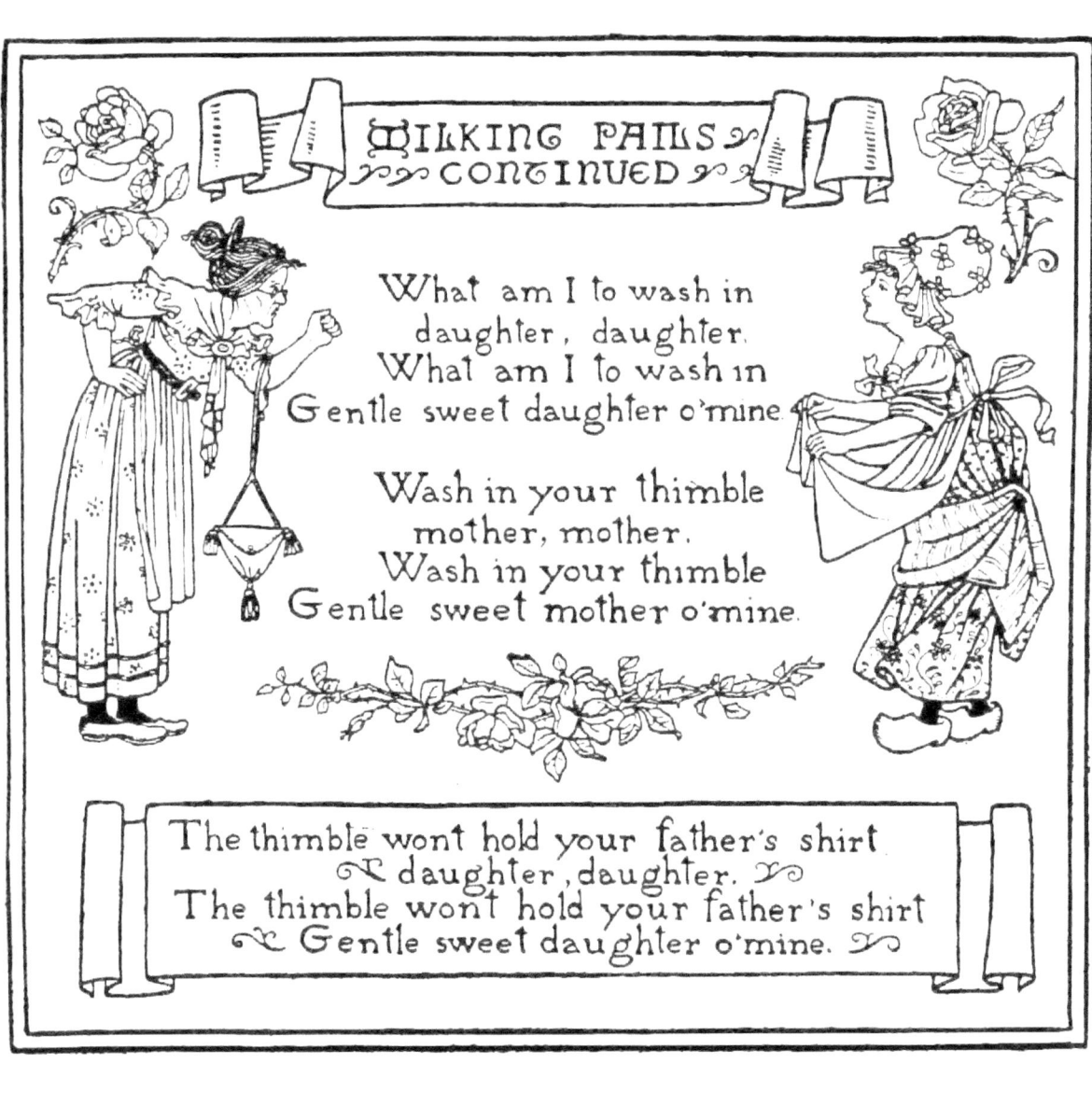

MILKING PAILS CONCLUDED

Set a man to watch them
    mother, mother.
Set a man to watch them
Gentle sweet mother o'mine.

Suppose the man should go to sleep
    daughter, daughter.
Suppose the man should go to sleep
Gentle sweet daughter o'mine.

Take a boat and go after them
    mother, mother.
Take a boat and go after them
Gentle sweet mother o'mine.

Suppose the boat should be upset
    daughter, daughter.
Suppose the boat should be upset
Gentle sweet daughter o'mine.

Then there would be an end of you
    mother, mother.
Then there would be an end of you
Gentle sweet mother o'mine.

OLD ROGER

They planted an apple tree over his head
H'm! ha!   over his head.

The apples were ripe and ready to drop
H'm! ha!   ready to drop.

There came an old woman a picking them up
H'm! ha!   picking them up.

Old Roger jumped up and gave her a knock
H'm! ha!   gave her a knock.

Which made that old woman go hippity hop
H'm! ha!   hippity hop.

OLD ROGER

We dont care for your men nor [you]
   Though you're the Rovers
We dont care for your men nor [you]
For we're the Guardian Soldiers.

We will send our dogs to bite
   We are the Rovers
We will send our dogs to bite
   Though you're the Guardian Soldiers.

We dont care for your dogs nor [you]
   Though you're the Rovers
We dont care for your dogs nor [you]
For we're the Guardian Soldiers.

Will you have a glass of wine
   We are the Rovers
Will you have a glass of wine
For respect of Guardian Soldiers.

WE ARE THE ROVERS

CONCLUDED

A glass of wine won't serve us all
    Though you're the Rovers,
A glass of wine won't serve us all
  For we're the Guardian Soldiers.

A barrel of beer won't serve us all
    Though you're the Rovers,
A barrel of beer won't serve us all
  For we're gallant Guardian Soldiers.

We don't fear your blue-coat men
    Though you're the Rovers,
We don't fear your blue-coat men
  For we're the Guardian Soldiers.

We don't mind your red-coat men
    Though you're the Rovers,
We don't mind your red-coat men
  For we're the Guardian Soldiers.

Will a barrel of beer then serve you all
  We are the Rovers,
Will a barrel of beer then serve you all
  As you're the Guardian Soldiers.

We will send our blue coat men
    We are the Rovers,
We will send our blue coat men
  Though you're the Guardian Soldiers.

We will send our red-coat men
    We are the Rovers,
We will send our red-coat men
  Though you're the Guardian Soldiers.

Are you ready for a fight
    We are the Rovers,
Are you ready for a fight
  Though you're the Guardian Soldiers.

Yes! we're ready for a fight
    Though you're the Rovers,
Yes! we're ready for a fight
  For we're the Guardian Soldiers
Present! Shoot! Bang! Fire.

Weitere Ausmalbücher von Luisa Rose:

Titel	ISBN
Alice im Wunderland	9783741297502
Blumen und Märchen	9783743102002
Der Struwwelpeter	9783743102699
Die Struwwelliese	9783743102811
Don Quixote	9783743104037
Drei kleine Schweine	9783743104099
Eine Blumenhochzeit	9783743104105
Fröhliche Reigenspiele	9783743104112
Lustige Tanzspiele	9783743104273
Reise ins antike Griechenland	9783743112568
Flucht ins antike Griechenland	9783743112599
Pariser Leben im 19.Jahrhundert	9783743112704
Die Sommerkönigin	9783743112742
Der Schneider und die Krähe	9783743112827
Die Wikinger	9783743113275
Hänsel und Gretel	9783743114265
Max und Moritz	9783743103214
Schnurrdirburr	9783743112834
Mode des 18. und 19. Jahrhunderts	9783743112971
Kostümbilder des 18. und 19. Jahrhunderts	9783743114401
Abenteuer im Bienenland	9783743117051
Griechische Helden der Antike	9783743117709
Märchen alter Zeit	9783743116559

Notizbücher von Luisa Rose:

Titel	ISBN
Drachentöter (Notizbuch)	9783743113077
Natures Wonders (Notizbuch)	9783743113817
Gedankenspiel Notizen (Notizbuch)	9783743113886
Smaragd Notizen (Notizbuch)	9783743114296
Jagd Notizen (Notizbuch)	9783743114302
Tradition (Notizbuch)	9783743114319
Antik Notizbuch (Notizbuch)	9783743114326
Veni Vidi Vici (Notizbuch)	9783743114340
Black List (Notizbuch)	9783743114371
Mystic Notes (Notizbuch)	9783743114388
Magic Notes (Notizbuch)	9783743114418
Fantasien (Notizbuch)	9783743114463
Creative Notes (Notizbuch)	9783743114487
Persönliche Notizen (Notizbuch)	9783743114494
Peter Pan (Notizbuch)	9783743114531
Rose (Notizbuch)	9783743114548
Quality Street (Notizbuch)	9783743114555
Rubin Notizen (Notizbuch)	9783743114647
Schmetterlinge (Notizbuch)	9783743114661
Ali Baba (Notizbuch)	9783743114678
The portrait of a Lady (Notizbuch)	9783743114692
Shakespeare (Notizbuch)	9783743114722
Brainstorming (Notizbuch)	9783743114739
Merlin (Notizbuch)	9783743114746
Rügen (Notizbuch)	9783743114784

Möchtest du über neue Bücher von Luisa Rose per email Informiert werden? Dann schicke eine Email mit ‚Newsletter' im Betreff an Luisa.Rose@t-online.de